SUPER SANDCASTLE™
It's the Alphabet!

It's Z!

Mary Elizabeth Salzmann

Consulting Editor, Diane Craig, M.A./Reading Specialist

Published by ABDO Publishing Company, 8000 West 78th Street, Edina, Minnesota 55439. Copyright © 2010 by Abdo Consulting Group, Inc. International copyrights reserved in all countries. No part of this book may be reproduced in any form without written permission from the publisher. Super SandCastle™ is a trademark and logo of ABDO Publishing Company.

Printed in the United States.

 PRINTED ON RECYCLED PAPER

Editor: Katherine Hengel
Content Developer: Nancy Tuminelly
Cover and Interior Design and Production: Kelly Doudna, Mighty Media
Photo Credits: iStockphoto (Jani Bryson), Shutterstock

Library of Congress Cataloging-in-Publication Data
Salzmann, Mary Elizabeth, 1968-
  It's Z! / Mary Elizabeth Salzmann.
    p. cm. -- (It's the alphabet!)
  ISBN 978-1-60453-613-3
  1. English language--Alphabet--Juvenile literature. 2. Alphabet books--Juvenile literature. I. Title.
  PE1155.S2698 2010
  421'.1--dc22
  ⟨E⟩
                                        2009022036

Super SandCastle™ books are created by a team of professional educators, reading specialists, and content developers around five essential components— phonemic awareness, phonics, vocabulary, text comprehension, and fluency—to assist young readers as they develop reading skills and strategies and increase their general knowledge. All books are written, reviewed, and leveled for guided reading, early reading intervention, and Accelerated Reader® programs for use in shared, guided, and independent reading and writing activities to support a balanced approach to literacy instruction.

About SUPER SANDCASTLE™

**Bigger Books for Emerging Readers
Grades K–4**

Created for library, classroom, and at-home use, Super SandCastle™ books support and engage young readers as they develop and build literacy skills and will increase their general knowledge about the world around them. Super SandCastle™ books are an extension of SandCastle™, the leading preK–3 imprint for emerging and beginning readers. Super SandCastle™ features a larger trim size for more reading fun.

Let Us Know
Super SandCastle™ would like to hear your stories about reading this book. What was your favorite page? Was there something hard that you needed help with? Share the ups and downs of learning to read. We want to hear from you! Send us an e-mail.

sandcastle@abdopublishing.com

Contact us for a complete list of SandCastle™, Super SandCastle™, and other nonfiction and fiction titles from ABDO Publishing Company.

www.abdopublishing.com • 8000 West 78th Street
Edina, MN 55439 • 800-800-1312 • 952-831-1632 fax

Aa Bb Cc Dd Ee
Ff Gg Hh Ii Jj Kk
Ll Mm Nn Oo Pp
Qq Rr Ss Tt Uu Vv
Ww Xx Yy Zz

The Letter

Zz

Z and z can also look like

Zz **Zz** Zz Zz Zz Zz

The letter **z** is a consonant.

It is the 26th letter of the alphabet.

Some words start with **z**.

zither

zipper

zebra

6

Zach

At the zoo, Zach sees
a zebra carrying a zither
in a bag with many zippers.

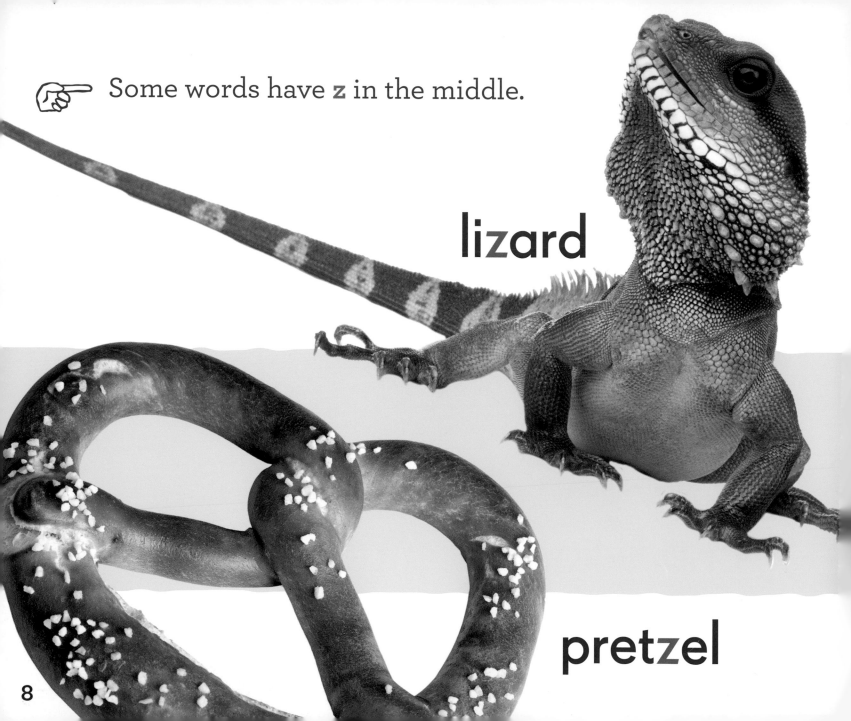

☞ Some words have **z** in the middle.

lizard

pretzel

8

Suzy

Suzy is amazed by the size of the pretzel the crazy lizard seized.

Some words end with **z**.

fez

quiz

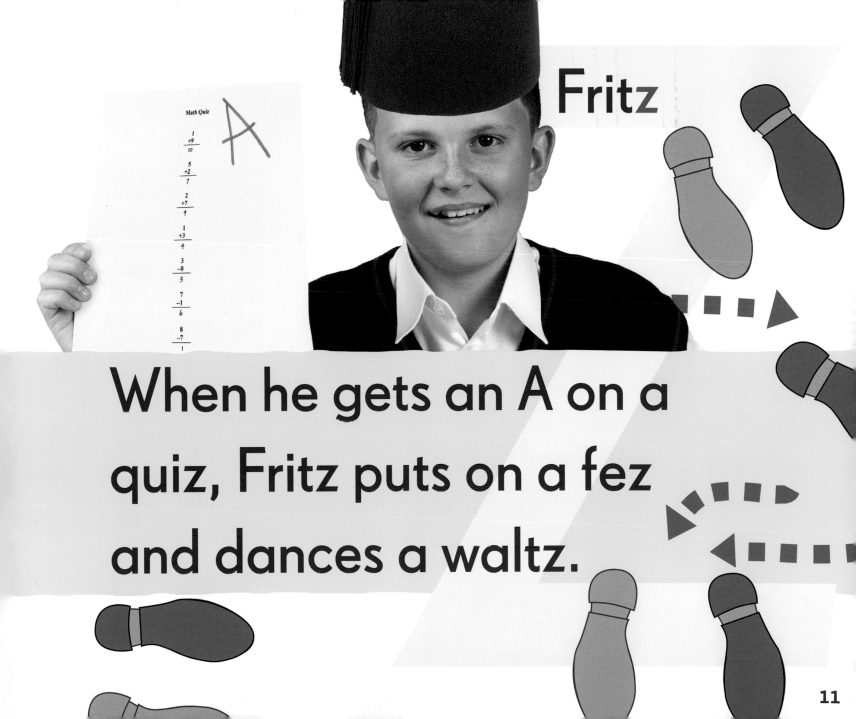

Math Quiz

$$\begin{array}{r} 1 \\ +9 \\ \hline 10 \end{array}$$

$$\begin{array}{r} 5 \\ +2 \\ \hline 7 \end{array}$$

$$\begin{array}{r} 2 \\ +7 \\ \hline 9 \end{array}$$

$$\begin{array}{r} 1 \\ +3 \\ \hline 4 \end{array}$$

$$\begin{array}{r} 3 \\ -0 \\ \hline 3 \end{array}$$

$$\begin{array}{r} 7 \\ -1 \\ \hline 6 \end{array}$$

$$\begin{array}{r} 8 \\ -7 \\ \hline 1 \end{array}$$

Fritz

When he gets an A on a quiz, Fritz puts on a fez and dances a waltz.

Some words have a double **z**.

grizzly bear

pizza

In the word *pizza*, it sounds like there is a t before the first z.

Lizzie

During blizzards, Lizzie and a fuzzy grizzly bear eat pizza and listen to jazz.

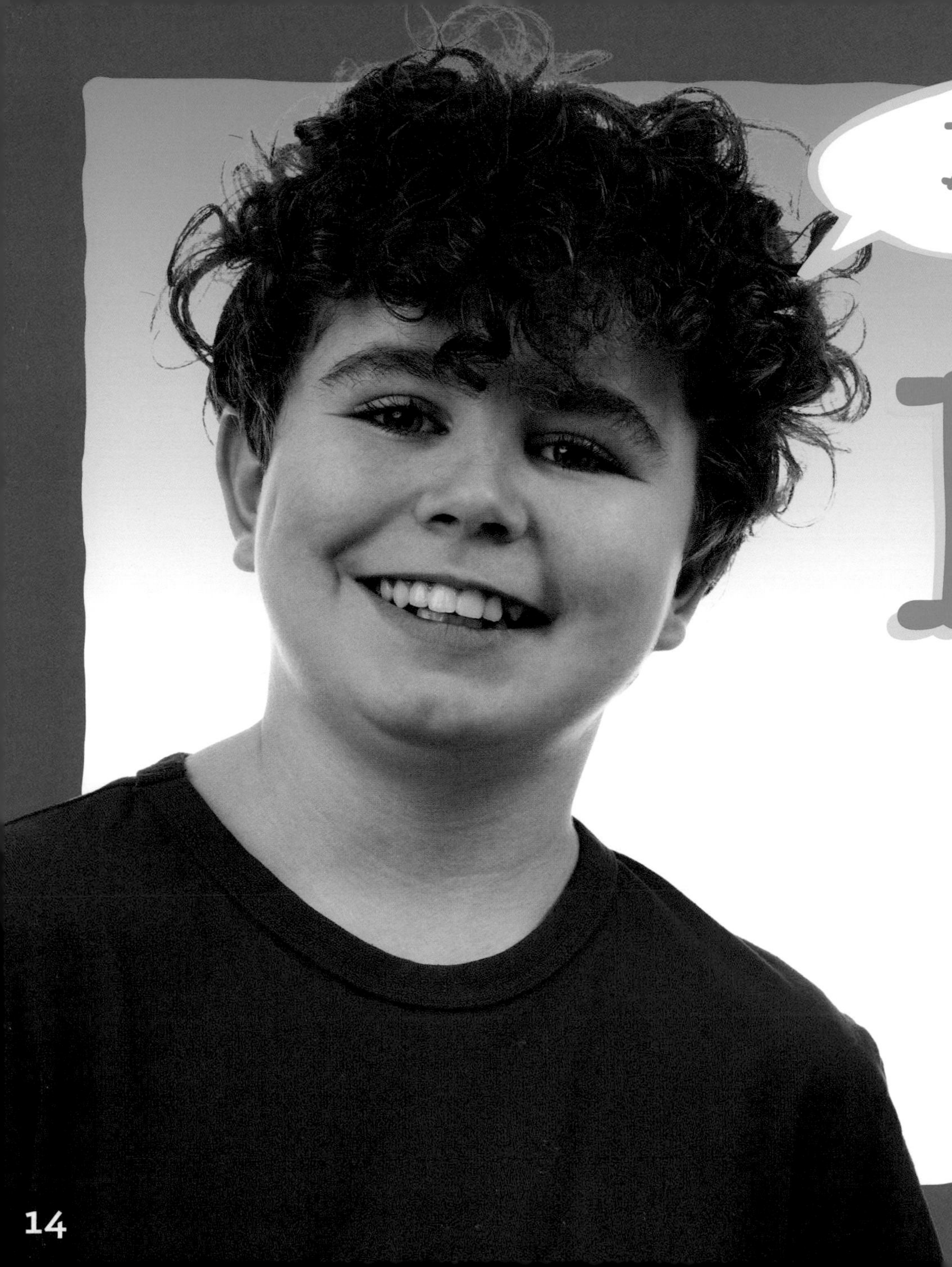

It's Z!

Zelly Zebra and Izzy Lizard
spend lazy days in the zoo.

They wake up after dozing
and need something to do.

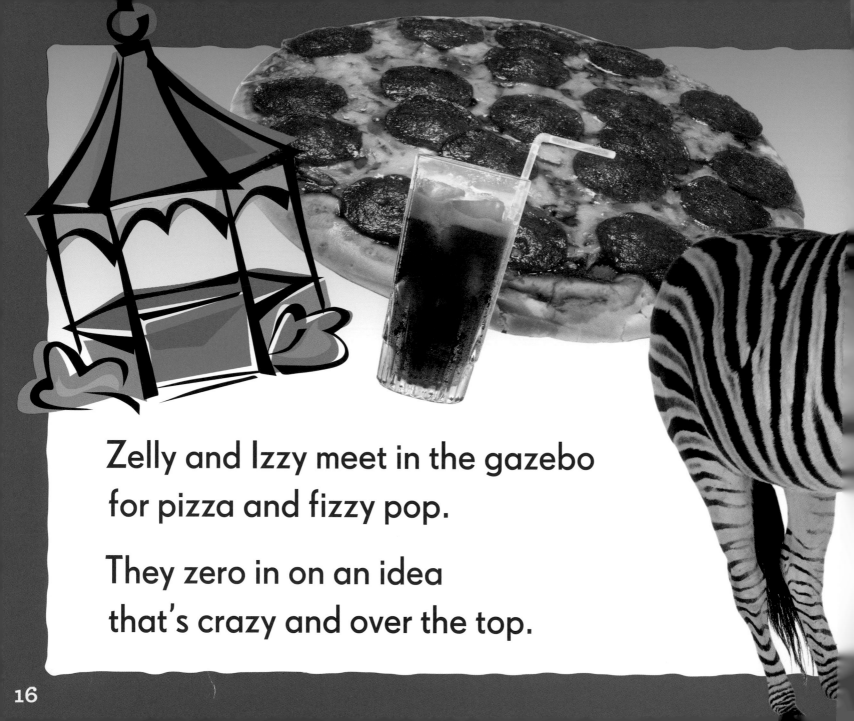

Zelly and Izzy meet in the gazebo
for pizza and fizzy pop.

They zero in on an idea
that's crazy and over the top.

"Let's zip around in a zeppelin
and zoom on the breeze.

We'll zig, and we'll zag,
and we'll go where we please!"

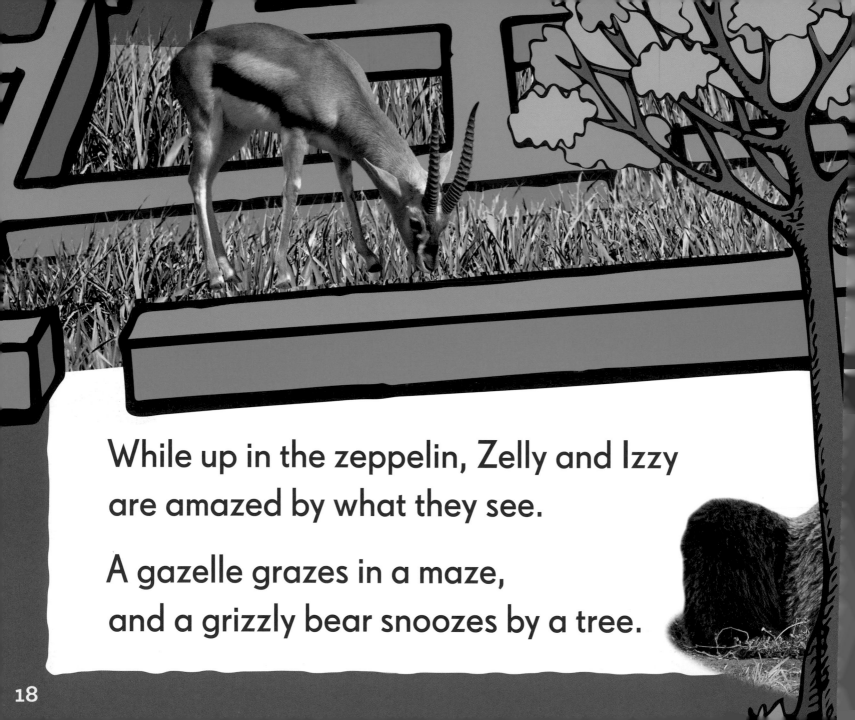

While up in the zeppelin, Zelly and Izzy
are amazed by what they see.

A gazelle grazes in a maze,
and a grizzly bear snoozes by a tree.

A chimpanzee on a bulldozer puts out a burning blaze.

Then he eats a glazed doughnut in the smoky haze.

Zelly and Izzy fly the zeppelin back home to the zoo.

They sigh, "Gee whiz!" and zonk out until two.

Which words have the letter **z**?

zipper

ladybug

zebra

pizza

penny

pretzel

rabbit

lizard

Glossary

fez (pp. 10, 11) – a red, brimless hat that is flat on top and has a tassel.

gazebo (p. 16) – a small building with open sides that is often in a park or garden.

glaze (p. 19) – a thin covering of icing.

graze (p. 18) – to eat growing grasses and plants.

jazz (p. 13) – an American style of music in which musicians often make up the tune as they play.

maze (p. 18) – a confusing series of connected paths.

waltz (p. 11) – a kind of ballroom dance.

zeppelin (pp. 17, 18, 20) – a large airship that has a metal frame.

zither (pp. 6, 7) – a musical instrument that has up to 40 strings stretched across a flat, hollow box.

To promote letter recognition, letters are highlighted instead of glossary words in this series. The page numbers above indicate where the glossary words can be found.

More Words with Z

Find the **z** in the beginning, middle, or end of each word.

bronze	hazel	puzzle	zap	zest
buzz	kazoo	realize	zeal	zigzag
citizen	klutz	recognize	zealous	zillion
cozy	magazine	unzip	zenith	zinc
dizzy	nuzzle	wizard	zephyr	zinnia
freeze	prize	zany	zero	zone